TOO CUTE PUPPIES

ISBN-13: 978-0-373-89286-0

Library of Congress Cataloging-in-Publication Data

Too cute puppies / Animal Planet's most impossibly adorable puppies.
    pages cm
  ISBN 978-0-373-89286-0 (hardback)
1. Puppies--Pictorial works.
I. Animal Planet (Television network)
  SF430.T66 2013
  636.7'07--dc23

                                          2013026787

too cute Puppies

Animal Planet's Most
Impossibly Adorable Puppies

Mamie, a **Labrador Retriever,** has been awaiting the arrival of her nine puppies for sixty-three days. After welcoming her lovable bundles of fur one by one, she takes a nap while the little ones enjoy dinner.

One look at this sweet face, and there is no question why the Labrador Retriever—an obvious overachiever in being adorable—is the world's most popular dog. Kramer doesn't know it yet, but he and his eight siblings are going to grow up to bring joy, slobbery kisses and even some much-needed help to the people in their lives.

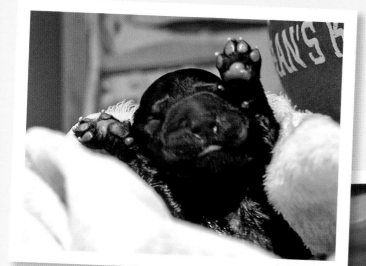

Teddy came into the world with his paws held high and a lot to say about his arrival. Even though he's a natural at being cute, Teddy has a lot to learn about his future profession as a Guide Dog for the Blind.

There is nothing sweeter than a pile of sleeping Labrador puppies.

Labrador Retrievers are hunting dogs that love nothing more than to romp in the open air. This is especially true of puppies like Kramer, who is just discovering what the outdoors offers in edible toys.

In the future, Teddy will have a life of responsibilities and a friend to look after, but for now, every day is a carefree play day.

Kramer, Teddy and their siblings will be grown soon, and they're eager to be accepted into the program at Guide Dogs for the Blind. Even grown up, there is no denying that they are just too cute.

Now that Kramer and Teddy are older, they have to learn to eat adult food. Rice cereal is even yummier when you share it with a sibling.

The **Rhodesian Ridgeback** is a breed known for hunting and running, but for now Peanut snoozes with her beloved puppies. Gemma and Clover don't yet know that they are going to be strong and muscular working dogs. Their only work now is to mesmerize everyone with their petite paws and crinkly noses.

Havanese, with their gorgeous hair and lofty airs, were once lap-dogs for Cuban aristocrats. Lulu is as pretty as a princess, and her five puppies are charming enough to entertain royalty.

Lulu's five puppies are adorably adorned with black-and-white spots, just like Mom. But huddled in the middle of the puppy pile is Misty, a rare pure-white Havanese. She is sure to be a royal jewel.

Just as royalty should, the Havanese puppies are enjoying their early days of leisure and lounging. After all, who would disturb anyone with such a delightful, furry face?

Portuguese Water Dogs are strong swimmers with waterproof coats. Domino, with fancy white gloves on his webbed feet, should be a natural at the dog paddle. From the looks of things, however, it's not exactly love at first swim. All the same, he's still a splash as a bathing beauty.

Ruby, a **Shih Tzu** with cover-girl locks and a supermodel smile, is a natural scene stealer wherever she makes an appearance. She isn't doing a lot of entertaining these days though; she's busy being a mother to her three darling girls.

Over 2,000 years ago, Tibetan monks bred this popular lap-dog to resemble lions. Sisters Kyra, Lola and Ruby Jr. don't quite look ready to roar, but they're definitely queens of cute!

Ruby Jr. is a natural blonde, just like her mother, and soon her short hairdo will grow into the long locks that make their breed famous. Still, she looks super sweet in her new puppy-do!

The girls are growing! With Mom and Dad outside playing, the puppies
are on a mission to discover the world. First item on the list: find a snack!

Staying beautiful takes a lot of work. A Shih Tzu's coat must be constantly maintained, but it's worth all the fluffing and primping to be this darling.

Now seven weeks old, Kyra, Lola and Ruby Jr. are looking perfectly precious and ready to meet new friends. In fact, Kyra is already saying, "Hello"!

Jack Russell Terriers were bred in the early nineteenth century to be fox hunters. Apple, Buttons and Cocoa are too busy posing to chase after foxes. But they could catch the love of just about anyone with their adorable mugs.

"Labradoodles" are a cross between the Labrador Retriever and the Standard Poodle. Both breeds are super swimmers, but these pretty puppies are just super snoozers. Rocky and Stanley are fun-loving pups that are going to be full of energy when they grow up…and wake up!

Mother Maya is proud of her twin boys. Don't let their sweet faces and teddy bear build fool you though. The two trouble-making boys keep Maya on her toes!

Oscar is twice as big as Tony, but what he lacks in size, Tony makes up for in bravery. When it comes to cute, however, it's a tie!

Chows are one of the first domesticated breeds of dogs. They originated in China, where they were bred to be hunting dogs. But Tony is so huggable that if he's looking for a cuddle, he won't have to hunt for one.

Bear is one of eleven **Rottweiler** pups and the runt of his litter. Size doesn't squelch his adventuresome spirit. While his babysitter is distracted, Bear decides to find out what's on the other side of the fence. Get ready, outside world! You're about to get a big dose of cute!

American Pit Bull Terriers are a cross between the English Bulldog and the English Terrier. Someday Thor will be a sleek, muscular dog weighing close to 100 pounds. Today, he's a pint-size package of precious.

While Mom, Venus, is out for some daily exercise, the eight siblings huddle together in a warm puddle of puppies. When you have this many siblings, there is always someone closeby to cuddle with.

Thor is always ready for a rousing wrestle, but his sister Gwen isn't quite ready to rouse.

Now that Thor is older, it's time for him to follow his mom on his first walk around the neighborhood. Looks like someone forgot to tell him that the whole point of walking is to, well … walk.

The Pit Bulls are eight weeks old, and every day is a rowdy puppy party.
It is almost time for them to wiggle their way into a new family's heart.

All of the Pit Bull puppies are going to their new homes, and it's almost Thor's turn. Pretty soon he will be meeting a little boy who thinks he is perfect, and it will be love at first cuddle.

Freddy, Suzy and Ivan are brand-new **Pugs,** a toy breed that originated in China. In 2004 a Pug won Best in Show at the World Dog Show. For now, these three are happy being photogenic on their own red carpet.

Ivan may be nothing more than an irresistible furry bump on the floor right now, but he is going to grow up to be an outgoing family dog with a big personality.

The **Chinese Crested** dog is best known as a mostly hairless breed, except for the trademark crest around their heads, plumed tails and furry socks. Buttons is of the "powderpuff" variety of the breed, which means he is entirely covered with a double-soft, straight coat. Whether or not he's showing skin, he's still a darling!

The **Cairn Terrier** is a hearty hunting dog but is perhaps best known for being the breed of dog that played "Toto" in *The Wizard of Oz*. Scout and her siblings create their own tornado of energy, and they know all about the magical world of cute!

There is nothing quite like a lazy afternoon spent spooning in the sun with your brothers and sisters. Three boy puppies and three girl puppies make for one irresistible six-pack.

The puppies are five weeks old and on their first outing. Growing up on a farm certainly has its benefits and adventures!

Scout is a true explorer. Cairn Terriers were bred to be tenacious in the hunt, but all that tenacity can be exhausting!

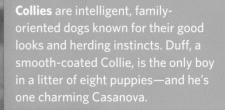

Collies are intelligent, family-oriented dogs known for their good looks and herding instincts. Duff, a smooth-coated Collie, is the only boy in a litter of eight puppies—and he's one charming Casanova.

Lassie, the most famous Collie on film and screen, was always off on an adventure. Penny loves adventure, too, but first she needs her beauty rest.

Collies have the largest vocabulary of any dog and are thought to understand more words their owners say than any other breed. So Penny likely knows exactly what you're saying when you tell her that her puppy face warms your heart.

Duff, showing off his striking sable coat, turns heads everywhere he goes.
And now that he is getting bigger, that's exactly where he goes...everywhere!

Collies love having plenty of room to roam. Now at six weeks old, for these Collie pups, the whole world is ripe for roaming!

All of the puppies have taken a personality test to help people choose the perfect homes for them. Penny's test showed that she is eager to please, but with her fuzzy paws and precious face, she doesn't have to work hard to please anyone.

Pancake and Raisin are **Chinese Shar-Pei** puppies, an ancient breed of Chinese guard dogs. Their loose skin was meant to stop attackers from getting a firm grip, but it wouldn't be hard to get a handful of these two dollops of darling—it would just be impossible to put them down!

Roxy, a **Dalmatian,** is the proud Mom of three peaceful and perfectly white pups, but they won't stay unspotted for long! Soon these puppies will have their racing spots and be running for adventure.

Sisters Francie and Madison are an inseparable duo, even though Madison is sometimes a late riser.

Dalmatians are an athletic and active breed, so Woodrow is always looking for a good time and a new toy.

Dalmatians are best known for their traditional role as firedogs. When the puppies are old enough to go to new homes, Woodrow is chosen to work at the local fire station. What a charmer!

It isn't hard to see why the **Cavalier King Charles Spaniel** was bred to be a king's companion. Tiny Paris is obviously highborn and precious.

These Cavaliers are always ready to make new friends, and they are wonderful with children and other dogs. Good thing, because the puppies are already irresistible.

Classified as a lap-dog, the Cavalier King Charles Spaniel is a bit more than a lapful, but Paris and her siblings are ready for a privileged life of leisure wherever they snooze!

There is nothing more curious than a Cavalier, and five-week-old Paris and her sister are ready to tackle the great outdoors. Hope the world is ready for a furry rush of cute!

This basket full of beauties is about to be set loose on the great outdoors. The grass is always greener when it's decorated with puppy paws.

Shy, petite Paris stays on the sidelines while her siblings discover the wilderness in their backyard. Turns out the outdoors is pretty tasty.

Paris is ready to go to her new home, where she is sure to sweep her new family off their feet!

The **Keeshond** is a breed from Holland and a larger cousin to the fluffy Pomeranian. These pups with their neatly furred faces will eventually have a thick, full coat that will lighten in color as they grow.

The **Cocker Spaniel** is one of the smallest of the sporting breeds, but Isabelle has five even smaller dogs on her mind: her five puppies. At five days old, they have a lot of growing to do.

Cocker Spaniels are thought to have come over to America on the *Mayflower* with the pilgrims. As members of a distinguished breed, Coffee and Midas would never wander about with wet fur without their loungewear.

Midas is the only golden puppy in his litter. He's easy to notice in a crowd, but he's not a pup that follows one. While his siblings are getting their first bath, he has snuck away.

Coffee is also experiencing his first bath, but he isn't too keen on getting clean. No matter how clean or dirty he is, though, you can't wash off the adorable.

Coco is a seven-day-old **French Bulldog.** With her short legs and even shorter snout, she's already a cuddly companion. She will grow up to follow her friends wherever they go, but until she masters her footing, she needs to rest up in order to grow up!

In a pack of eight **Alaskan Malamutes,** someone is going to grow up to be leader. Klondike is the leader of irresistible for now.

◀ These puppies will train together and learn to work as a sled dog team. They are already an eight-pack of adorable and inseparable fur balls.

Klondike and Avalanche are already competing to see who will be the pack leader. Klondike explains that the pack leader has the most to say in any situation. ▶

Malamutes communicate with pack mates through howls that can carry up to six miles. Klondike is already working on his howl harmonies.

Named for the Alaskan Mahlemut tribe, this breed is well known as a sled dog. Klondike may look tiny now, but someday he'll be able to pull as much as 3,000 pounds on a sled.

No snow? No problem. Pulling tires across the grass is a great exercise for sled dogs.

Already learning to wear a harness, the Malamute pups are well on their way. Draft dogs are happiest when they are working, but sometimes the nap in between is just as sweet.

Coton de Tulear means "cottony coat" in French. These well-dressed dogs, with their happy-go-lucky attitude, are the belles of every ball. Buttermilk is no exception. He's a social butterfly and already working on introducing himself to everyone he can meet.

Dachshund means "badger dog" in German, but these long and low dogs are often called "hot dogs."

The average Dachshund litter has four pups, but Rollo's litter is a double batch. At three weeks old, their eyes are open, but just barely.

Rollo is a small dog with a big sense of wonder. A speedy Dachshund was the mascot for the 1972 Olympics, and like that Dachshund, Rollo is ready to run!

Rollo is not too sure about running in costume, however. His Mom, Tina, may be a champion racer in the Hot Dog Bun Fun Run, but Rollo is wondering what's so fun about it—while looking adorable in the process.

Boxers are named for their ability to stand on their hind legs and appear to box, but they're more lovers than fighters. Peanut, the runt of his litter, may be small, but he's got a big heart and a heartbreaker's face.

In this litter of eight **Golden Retriever** puppies, one dog will be chosen to follow in their mother's champion paw prints and into the show ring. Ricky may not be ready for the show ring, but he already has a face that captivates.

Sophie is the mother of Ricky and the rest of their distinguished family of gorgeous blondes. An athlete as well as a superstar, she is taking some time off to focus on her puppies.

The road to glory as a show dog has to start somewhere, and step one is coming when called. Ricky, the biggest puppy of the litter, may be the first on his feet.

The puppies are teething, and nothing is safe from chewing, not even brothers and sisters—or in Ricky's case, spoons.

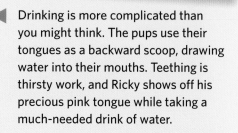

Drinking is more complicated than you might think. The pups use their tongues as a backward scoop, drawing water into their mouths. Teething is thirsty work, and Ricky shows off his precious pink tongue while taking a much-needed drink of water.

Ricky is chosen as pick of the litter and has big shoes to fill, but he has a different idea of how to fill them. No matter! He is already a show-stopper.

German Shepherds are legendary service dogs. However, puppies will be puppies, and Sawyer has wandered off on his first solo adventure. Fortunately, he is just as smart as he is handsome, and he is on his way back home.

Delta is two years old and has had her first litter of three puppies. They will be 115 pounds when they are fully grown, but weighed less than two pounds when they were born. They still have a lot of growing to do!

The **Bullmastiff** is one of the largest breeds, and Cesar is the biggest boy in his litter. Someday he'll be a fine guard dog, but until then he makes for a perfect furry friend.